Love Letters From The IRS

The Insider's Guide To Resolving & Preventing Tax Problems

Skylar Dubrow, CPA

CPAofThousandOaks.com

ISBN: 1507806892
ISBN-13: 978-1507806890

IMPORTANT NOTICE

While every effort has been taken to ensure that the information contained herein is accurate as of the time of publication, tax laws and regulations are constantly changing.

This book is designed to provide accurate and authoritative information in regards to the subject matter covered, but it is sold with the understanding that the publisher is not engaged in rendering legal or accounting services, and no information contained herein should be construed as legal advice. For personalized tax and accounting advice relevant to your specific situation, please contact the author directly at (818) 889-7285.

If legal advice or other expert assistance is required, the services of a competent professional person should be sought. The publisher does not guarantee or warrant that readers who use the information provided in this publication will achieve results similar to those discussed.

Contents

Introduction: Getting To Know Your New CPA

Hello, I am Skylar Dubrow, and I am your tax professional and business confidant. I am a Certified Public Accountant and I own and operate a successful CPA firm located in beautiful, sunny southern California. I have been legally saving families and businesses thousands of dollars every year through my unique approach to tax planning and business management, all while keeping my clients under the government radar.

Sometimes, we are called to stand up for our clients, and standing up for them with iron clad documentation is my strategy when the IRS comes a knocking.

My firm specializes in offering our clients *Five-Star Customer Service* in assisting with income tax matters, business startups, organization, ongoing tax compliance, and IRS and other government agency representation.

My passion for numbers started at the age of 12 when I was diagnosed with Type 1 diabetes. I was constantly playing numbers games and doing quick math calculations in my head. Looking at various ratios, averages, patterns, and triggers; budgeting my insulin for the sugar I ate. Which, come to find out later, is very similar to budgeting your income for the money you spend.

My original plan in life was to get my CPA license and then go work for the IRS for a few years. I figured that I would make some connections, go through their training, get that experience, on the assumption that this experience and training would be beneficial for my future clients in private practice.

However, life didn't happen that way.

I was highly involved in all sorts of activities, such as motorcycle riding, boating, wakeboarding, snowboarding, playing guitar. I was competing in all sorts of local amateur events and competitions for these activities. I met a lot of people in these various scenes, from fellow enthusiasts to the business owners that would put these events on.

Through all my social connections, by the time I had my CPA license, I already had a nice sized income tax preparation and bookkeeping business, which was growing at a nice pace. I decided to forgo the IRS career and continue to work side-by-side with my father and at the same time grow my own business on the side.

Living A Passionate Life

I have always been a passionate guy. For as long as I can remember, when I picked a new hobby, or a new activity, I always go the extreme. I read everything there is to know on the subject, watch all the related videos on the subject, and I master the technique or skill through repetitive practice. I am a firm believer in, "Practice makes perfect, practice makes permanent."

I am a firm believer that any type of great skill is only achieved through a significant time investment. I am constantly looking for better and more efficient ways of utilizing that time, however.

Growing up, I was always so passionate about skateboarding, wake boarding and snowboarding, roller hockey, playing the guitar, the cool stuff. It is surprising to some that I ended up playing in the income tax & business management game!

Looking back, I really feel that it worked out for the best this way.

Not only do I enjoy exploring my passions to the max, I enjoy sharing them with other people. I love to share my ideas and points of view with other people so much, it's probably safe to say I enjoy sharing them with new people more than I enjoy doing them by myself.. I really enjoy sharing shortcuts, tips, and life hacks that can really only be learned through experience.

I feel that is what lead me most to start writing this book. I wanted to put down some solid information that others can use to navigate the tricky territory of the IRS.

This book is a collection of my knowledge, strategies, and experience for dealing with the world's biggest collection agency: The Internal Revenue Service.

The reason for financial organization is to pursue your own passions. To me, life should be about pursuing your passions.

These are my passions, this is what life is about for me.

What are your passions? Perhaps it's running your business profitably and successfully. I'm here to help you with that, and keeping the IRS off your back so you can keep what is actually yours and not spend all your hard earned money on interest and penalties. You should be having time to enjoy doing the things you love, not having to deal with the government.

These are my passions, If you share one of them with me, I really want to meet you. Even if you don't, I would love to hear about yours and what I have been missing.

Family & Business

I grew up working with my father on all types of businesses, including furniture manufacturers, commercial installers, real estate, installations, entertainment (including adult!), everything you can think of. All of these businesses have one big thing in common: *Dealing with the IRS and other bureaucratic agencies is scary, time consuming, difficult, and burdensome.*

Budgeting for taxes can be downright devastating for some businesses. As I would assist and shadow my father, as we would visit his clients and discuss their affairs, I would admire how they would all look up to him and appreciate him and his valuable input so much. These were all very smart and successful businessmen that were looking up to my father for business-related advice. That is one of the many things that attracted me to this business. I enjoyed the advising, guidance, and authoritative direction.

While growing up working in my father's CPA firm, I was commonly asked, “Are you going to follow in your father's footsteps?"

My becoming a CPA was always an option, for as long as I can remember. Then, after having a few different jobs as a teenager, I worked as a pool service man, I worked as a private carnival engineer, then I managed a retail store.

At these physical labor jobs, I would have to take breaks to check and adjust my blood sugar, then wait for it to get back on target. All the while, my coworkers and teammates were waiting for me or would have to work without me. I had to make a really responsible decision. It was not before long that I realized I would need to find some other occupation that would allow me the convenience of being able to take care of these things when needed, and this manual labor road was not going to work out for me. That’s when accounting and taxation started looking really good. So from then on, I was on a mission to become a CPA, and most likely follow in my father's footsteps.

Being Young In The Tax Game
When I first started, I come across young entrepreneurs all the time who had great ideas and the means to be successful, but they never had any guidance on how to run a business in our highly bureaucratic world. I found myself talking to these young people who were having serious issues with the IRS and California Franchise Tax Board.

As a result of this early experience with young business people, who typically had no training and were not running their businesses properly, I was put in a position of teaching and coaching – just like I saw my father doing with his clients.

While working at my father's side, his idea of a "raise" was to give me some of his clients to assist. It turned out that these were typically his problem clients, or clients that needed a little more "hand holding". Working with these clients gave me a wide range of valuable experience, such as dealing with IRS and FTB tax controversies, audits, penalty abatements, amending returns, and other difficult subject matter.

Another type of client that I would happen to get often through my father were elderly clients. Individuals and married couples 80 years old and older. These are typically simple tax returns, and don't take very much time to complete. Because of this, I would use the extra time with these clients as an opportunity to ask them about all their tax prep experiences during their 60 years of filing tax returns.

What a great opportunity for me to get an inside look at a consumer who has experienced many different tax preparers. To talk to someone who has sat through 60 different tax prep appointments in their life, and ask them what they liked, did not like, and what they want out of a tax guy was both fascinating and enlightening. I was definitely taking notes, and have used that information to create my five-star customer service experiences today.

Diabetes and Me

Being diagnosed with Type 1 diabetes at a young age provided a series of early life lessons that continue to help me and my accounting clients to this day. Being a Type 1 diabetic has introduced me to a large, tight-knit community, and this has impacted how I work with others to this day.

Being forced to manage my blood sugar and other health factors gave me an early introduction to record keeping, budgeting, and planning. It taught me to be responsible, have discipline, do things in moderation at a young age.

Growing up as the only person I knew with this disease lead me to be a leader of my own life, not follow the crowd. I constantly had to make decisions for myself that were against all my peers. I also learned to have a deep and sincere compassion for other people. You never know what somebody else has gone through in their own life, or is going through right now.

Most people have struggles or are struggling with some aspect of their life. We are all different and have had different life experiences. A smiling face, or a helping hand can really go a long way.

This same passion that I feel for people is one of the things I love about my profession. I enjoy talking with people about this very important aspect of their life. With tax preparation and business consulting, I love learning how my clients live their life, how they make ends meet, the things that make them happy, their goals, dreams, plans for the future, and experiences from the past.

The Two-Wheeled Life

Motorcycle riding was something I got into in my mid-twenties. I am thankful that I waited for adulthood to start riding, as I was much smarter and less likely to do something stupid on a bike.

Being the extreme sport freak that I am, I of course went to one of the fastest, most aggressive motorcycles available: A beautiful black and white 2007 Honda CBR 600. At the time, I Lived on Malibu canyon just north of the 101 freeway. The famous Mulholland Canyon was my commute to work when our office was in Woodland Hills, on Topanga Canyon Blvd.

I could be sitting on my couch, and then, within 15 minutes, be suited up in full leathers charging the canyons. I rode those canyons almost every weekday. When I felt brave enough, I rode on weekends, too. I really loved the science and technicality of maneuvering my sport bike through the canyons, calculating just the right entry and exit points from each curve. There was a peaceful flow of motion that was exhilarating.

The most amazing thing about motorcycles is that there is not much to interrupt your thoughts. There is no radio to change channels, no way of answering a cell phone, no windows to roll up, and no traffic to stop for.

Just kidding about the traffic part. I was a very safe rider and always kept my distance. My strategy on the road was to get the hell away from everyone. When planning my business and brainstorming ideas to better serve my clients and be more efficient, I would often take to the canyons to escape distractions and clear my head.

Coincidentally enough, along Mulholland Canyon there are lots of pull over view sites. Fellow motorcyclists would stop in their travels, to stretch, recharge, and enjoy the scenery. I have met many of my close friends and clients at these motorcycle hangout spots. There is something about being a motorcycle rider that connects you instantly to another motorcycle rider. Even if they are into a different type of riding style, the passion for the sport is a unique one, it takes a certain type of individual to ride motorcycle. I really enjoy helping my fellow motorcycle enthusiasts with their tax and business issues.

The Right Way To Do Things

Whenever we are talking about taxes, personal finances, and operating a business, there are many ways to do things, but there are right ways to do them, and there are wrong ways to do them.

There are a few reasons why people do things the wrong way. Some people just do not know the right way. They have never been sat down and explained the proper way to do things. Or the situation has never arisen in their personal experience. Some people intentionally do things the wrong way out of laziness, or they feel that it's not a high priority.

However, there are far more benefits to doing things the right way. They are called the *right way* for a reason. And that is because out of all the ways of doing things, the right way solves more problems than any other way.

What it comes down to is taking a pro-active approach to your financial decisions and tax matters. Remember, documentation is everything. If you're going to take deductions and credits on your tax return, for example, there is a right way to do it, and a wrong way to do it.

Continuing with this example, if a particular deduction or credit is dependent on the amount of money you spend (as most of them are), it's vital to have a system in place to help you document those expenses throughout the year. But, it needs to be a system that works for you – something you'll actually use.

By documenting every transaction that will qualify for these deductions or credits, you are proactively preparing your supporting documents that you will need to defend yourself in the unlikely event of an audit situation.

Helping my clients establish systems like this that they'll both stick with and that meet government requirements is something I thoroughly enjoy working on. Although this is a simple example, I hope it illustrates the time, care, and commitment I dedicate to my clients.

It is my hope that this introduction shows you what has shaped my attitudes and beliefs about client service and bringing value to your personal and business life. I look forward to getting to know you and helping to make your life easier. Please give my office a call at (818) 889-7285 to schedule an appointment.

Chapter 1: Self-Employment Taxes

For most small business owners that have not set up a separate business entity, such as an LLC or corporation, one of the first (and biggest) tax surprises that they encounter are self-employment taxes.

When you work a job as an employee, you're probably already aware of the Social Security and Medicare taxes that come out of your paycheck. What you may not be aware of, however, is that the part that you see missing from your paycheck is actually only half of the total IRS bill for Social Security and Medicare taxes. The other half of this bill is paid directly by your employer. When you're self-employed, you are serving as both employee and employer. In such a situation, congratulations! You get to pay both halves. This is self-employment tax.

Social Security and Medicare taxes combined are going to eat up 15.3% of your self-employment profits. Fortunately, there is a $118,500 cap on the profits you have to pay this tax on (for 2015), but this is of little comfort if your profits are less than this amount.

If you have additional employees in your business, you also need to understand that you're going to be paying one half of their Social Security and Medicare taxes. In this case, they are called "employment taxes". There are also going to be additional taxes you pay for each employee, such as unemployment tax (which pays for unemployment benefits for layed off workers), worker's compensation insurance (in case of workplace injuries). In general, you should budget about 10% of an employee's salary for overhead to pay these additional taxes and insurance.

Now, back to self-employment taxes. You are responsible to take not only the employees portion but you are responsible to pay the full portion to the government on your earnings.

I know that 15.3% seems pretty high. Keep in mind that we are not talking about income taxes here. We are literally only talking about Social Security and Medicare. One of the nice things about being self-employed is you don't have to pay that 15.3% on everything that you earn. Rather, you only pay that on the profit that you end up showing from your business.

Let's take a look at a quick example. Let's say that you have a total of $100,000 worth of revenue for the year in your small business. But, you also have expenses associated with running your business. Let's say that you have $25,000 worth of expenses. That leaves $75,000 in profit.

You will only be required to pay self-employment tax on this $75,000.

Self-employment tax is a shocker to many people. Many small business owners that didn't seek proper advisement from somebody such as myself may find them blindsided by the tax bill associated with this self-employment tax.

But the good news is that with proper planning and budgeting it doesn't have to be such a sticker shock to us. We can actually budget for it, we could work this additional expense into our prices, and plan for it and treat it as an ordinary business expense and continue running our business and continue paying what we need to pay.

When properly budgeted and planned for, you should be paying into your self-employment tax bill four times per year. The IRS requires you to estimate your income for the year. This can be difficult, but there are guidelines for doing this. In general, these estimates are based on your previous year's income. Then, throughout the year you make estimated tax payments to pay both your self-employment taxes AND your estimated income taxes (since there is also nobody else sitting there withholding income taxes from your paycheck!).

Since this estimation process CAN be fairly difficult, especially if your income is seasonal, the IRS allows us to simplify the process and apply a set of "safe harbor" rules. This allows us to generalize our estimated expenses or estimated taxes and not have to pin-point it exactly when we send in the estimated amount. Our goal is to get the amount as close to accurate as possible for when we file the tax return, and this planning process is critical for the self-employed individual. This process is something that we would be happy to assist you with.

The IRS will impose penalties if you fail to make these estimated tax payments, or if the estimates are too low. The 10% underpayment penalty is one more thing that we can help you to avoid.

As we mentioned earlier, if you are an employee, your employer pays half the Social Security and Medicare bill on your behalf. Then, they get to deduct that as a business expense on their business return.

Fortunately, under the current tax rules, you get to do the exact same thing. Even though you still have to pay the full amount of the self-employment tax, you get to deduct one-half of this amount from your taxable income for purposes of calculating your income tax bill.

So that's the federal government. We also have the state to worry about.

The complexity of your state situation will obviously vary depending upon your state of residence. Some states don't have a state income tax, but all states have unemployment insurance that needs to be paid. Here in California, where my accounting firm is based, we have some of the most extensive and complicated state tax reporting requirements in the nation.

The percentages that are charged by all states are going to be less than the federal government, but can still be quite substantial. They need to be treated with the same seriousness as IRS taxes, and should not be ignored. As part of this process, you're going to be paying estimated taxes to the state, also. Most states have aligned their estimated tax payment deadlines with the IRS dates, so that you can just do it at the same time.

Many businesses will forget to take into account the impact of state taxes when creating their budgets (for those that bother to budget!). This is an important conversation to have with your tax professional.

Chapter 2: Saving Taxes With Entities

In the last chapter, we discussed the tax situation for self-employed individuals. That discussion applies to small businesses that have chosen not to create a legal entity separate from themselves.

The absolute most simple business structure to set up is the sole proprietorship. The terms self-employed and sole proprietor mean the exact same thing – especially from a tax perspective.

On the federal side, you don't need to do anything special to create a sole proprietorship. As far as the IRS is concerned, as long as you pay those self-employment taxes and file the extra forms required with your personal income tax return, you're in business.

Of course, your state, county, and even city may have additional requirements. The most common requirements are to obtain a local business license and to register a trade name (also known as a DBA – "doing business as").

There are a lot of downsides to operating as a sole proprietor. While beyond the scope of this book, this business type has the greatest liability exposure for the owner. This form of operation also incurs the highest personal tax bill, as we discussed in the last chapter.

A better way to operate is to create a business entity that is legally separate and distinct from yourself as an individual. The most common types of legal entities that you may be familiar with include corporations, partnerships, and the new-fangled LLC (limited liability company).

What this is technically doing is we are now separating your business activity from your own personal self. There are several advantages to creating this sort of separation, including a lot of little things you wouldn't normally consider/

Far and away the two biggest reasons for creating the separate entity, however, are the liability protection and the tax planning benefits.

Let's look at the liability factor. If I offer a delivery service business and I happen to get into an accident, the other person may sue the business. If there is no legal separation between myself and the business, then they are going to be suing me personally. If I have an LLC or corporation, however, they may be limited to just suing the company, providing a layer of protection for myself personally.

The level of risk of your business activity is something you should discuss with an asset protection attorney in order to help determine the best type of business entity for you from this perspective.

Let's talk about the tax side of things. It's pretty common these days to hear people talking about LLCs. This is the most common business entity type to hear about on the radio, TV, and online. The reality is that an LLC isn't for everybody, and it may not be the right type of business entity for you.

More often than not, an LLC is really geared, in my opinion, for either small businesses that won't end up doing much in gross sales or rental properties. In my experience, many businesses are much better off being run as corporations, and they are very similar to an LLC in some regards, but the filing and reporting requirements are a little bit different.

Regardless of whether it's an LLC or a corporation we're talking about, the liability protection is very similar, if done properly. It should also be noted that, while overall audit risk is pretty low either way, your audit is actually lower with an LLC or corporation than it is for a sole proprietorship. This is just one more benefit to setting up the proper entity for your business.

The reason for this is because these business entities are going to have greater reporting requirements than a sole proprietorship. For example, you may be required to report a balance sheet – meaning that you are required to report your assets and debts. This is never required in a sole proprietorship situation.

Due to these enhanced reporting requirements, the IRS

often just assumes that everything is going to be reported correctly. This is especially true because of the assumption that more complicated businesses are going to use the services of a professional accountant, such as myself.

When you operate a separate entity, as already mentioned, you're going to have some more reporting and filing requirements. For an LLC or corporation, you're going to have a separate tax return filed for that particular business. Then, the business is going to issue a form K-1 to you personally for use in filing your personal income tax return. This K-1 is similar to a W-2 or 1099 in some regards, but contains a lot more information and can be much more complicated.

In addition, depending on how your company is structured, you may also be set up as an employee of your own company, and thus receive aW-2.

If you set up an LLC and you are the only owner, the IRS will actually classify you as a self-employed, sole proprietorship. This is because under federal law, there is no specific tax treatment for LLCs.

If you create your LLC with two or more owners (technically called "members"), then you will be classified by the IRS as a partnership by default.

These default classifications are usually not in your best interest. For example, accepting the default classification of sole proprietorship or partnership for an LLC does not eliminate the self-employment tax issue.

At the same time, we want to avoid the double taxation element of having a corporation. The double taxation problem arises because, for regular corporations, the corporate entity itself is required to pay income tax on any profits. Then, when these profits are passed on to the owners (shareholders) in the form of dividends, you have to pay personal income tax on that money *again*.

In order to avoid this, most small businesses will opt to be treated as a *small corporation*, referred to as a "subchapter S corporation" for the section of the law that creates this special tax classification. An S-corporation is a pass through entity, meaning that all profits are passed through directly to the owners, rather than being taxed at the entity level. This entirely eliminates the double taxation problem.

Choosing to be treated as an S-corporation is completely optional. In order to elect to be treated this way, you must file IRS Form 2553. There are specific requirements that need to be met in order to file this form, and it can only be done at certain times of the year.

In my experience, the S-corp structure is the best for the vast majority of small businesses. The nice thing about the S-corp is that just about any entity type can select this election. For example, a single owner LLC, a two owner LLC, a 5 owner LLC, and a corporation can all choose to be treated as an S-corporation.

There are specific rules that all S-corporations must meet. For example, they are not allowed to have more than 25 owners, members, or shareholders. There are additional rules regarding the fiscal year of the business, foreign investors, and more. Please call my office at (818) 889-7285 to schedule an appointment to discuss your particular situation and see if you are eligible to elect S-corp status.

For many single-member LLCs, choosing S-corp status can easily save you up to $15,000 per year, even after taking into account the slight increase in your administrative costs associated with the increased reporting requirements for the S-corp. This one thing might prove to be the best tax planning strategy you every use!

There is one particular requirement of this S-corp strategy that, for some reason, tends to scare some people. Any owners of the S-corp that actively participate in the operation of the business are required to draw some form of paycheck from the business.

The reason for this requirement is simple. As an S-corp, you pay no self-employment taxes on profits that are passed through to you. In fact, you don't pay ANY Social Security and Medicare taxes, period, on any of that pass-through profit. This is actually why we use the S-corp – to save on those exact taxes.

Unfortunately, we can't do this for every dime we take from the company. Part of the same section of law that created this beautiful S-corp benefit was also a requirement that it can't be used to avoid paying all Social Security and Medicare taxes – otherwise nobody would pay them!

The actual money that today's retired seniors paid in to this system their entire life is long gone. All Social Security and Medicare benefits for current recipients is actually paid for by the people that are currently working and paying these taxes. Thus, the IRS is very concerned about the payment and collection of these taxes, because it's what keeps the system going for people currently collecting Social Security benefits.

In order to make sure that all small business owners are paying their fair share into the Social Security and Medicare Trust Funds (these monies are often called "trust fund taxes" by the IRS), everybody at the business is required to be paid *reasonable compensation*, including owners and shareholders.

The definition of what constitutes a "reasonable" paycheck for an S-corp small business owner is one of the most frequently and hotly contested issues every year in tax court. Every year, there are many reasonable compensation cases that go in front of the tax courts, and many more end up in audit situations.

We mentioned earlier that S-corps have lower audit rates than sole proprietorships. The one exception to this, however, is S-corps that don't pay reasonable compensation to their owners. If you want to get audited, this is the fastest way to ensure it happens!

When you pay yourself wages or salary from the business, you pay into Social Security and Medicare. The business still gets to deduct it's half of that money on the corporate return.

So how does this save you money? Let's say your business generates $100,000 in bottom line profit. For what you do, let's say that $50,000 is a "reasonable" salary for yourself. In this example, a self-employed person is going to pay 15.3% self-employment tax on the full $100,000 in profit. The S-corp owner, on the other hand, is only going to pay that tax on the $50,000 in salary. The other $50,000 in profit still requires payment of income tax, but you save that 15.3%. In this example, that's a savings of $7,650 in one year!

So how much salary do you have to take in order to be reasonable, and avoid any risks? This will depend on a LOT of factors, but common things to take into consideration include the salary for somebody in your area doing a similar job, the number of hours you actually work, the responsibilities you take on versus other staff members, and more.

Let's go back to why many business owners don't want to pay themselves a salary (aside from not wanting to pay ANY Social Security taxes!). If you don't currently have any other employees, you're going to need to create a payroll system for just yourself, and this can be quite burdensome.

You're not only going to have to start filing five new tax returns each year to the IRS, but you're also going to have state reporting requirements (unless you live in one of the few states without a state income tax). You're also going to have to make frequent (usually monthly) payments to the IRS and state to pay over those employment taxes.

This extra burden of having a proper payroll process is daunting to most people. Fortunately, an entire industry exists in this country that allows you to outsource this service for a very reasonable fee. Finding the right *payroll processor* to handle all aspects of this for you is quick and painless – and then YOU don't have to worry about it!

Hiring a payroll service for just one employee is very affordable, and worth doing to have it done right. This does eat into the tax savings, of course, but you still come out ahead. Paying a few hundred dollars per year for a payroll service is more than worth being able to save THOUSANDS on your tax bill.

Please call my office directly at (818) 889-7285 to discuss how an S-corp can save you money, and to discuss setting up your payroll processing.

Chapter 3: Minimizing Your Tax Bill Starts With Your Tax Returns

Penalties and interest are calculated as percentage of your tax liability. The less you owe on your actual tax returns, the less you owe overall. In a later chapter, we'll discuss the process of replacing SFR's and filing unfiled returns, but first, let's cover the tax return process itself and how to minimize your tax liability. The majority of this chapter will cover how to minimize taxes on your personal income tax return, but the end of this chapter will include a section on minimizing your liability for other tax types, particularly Form 941 employment taxes for businesses.

Your Personal Income Tax Return (1040)

There are numerous books published every tax season promising you how to keep your tax bill to an absolute minimum, and they want you to buy a new such book every year. The dirty little secret of the "annual tax savings book industry", however, is that their books are usually nothing more than heavily annotated reprintings of IRS Publication 17, which is the IRS handbook for filing a personal income tax return.

These published books, and Pub 17, walk through the entire process of preparing a tax return, including every form, schedule, and worksheet that gets attached to your Form 1040. Publication 17 is available for free from your local IRS office, or you can download a PDF from irs.gov.

My purpose in this chapter is not to go through every bit of Pub 17 and regurgitate it. As I already mentioned, there are plenty of other books out there that have already done that. In this chapter, I want to present the main ideas behind how your tax bill is computed, and what goes into minimizing it.

Income

First, let's look at the one item that has the biggest impact on your personal income tax: Your income. Income has an extremely broad definition in the Internal Revenue Code. Essentially, any time you experience a financial gain of any sort, the government considers it income, with a few limited exceptions.

Money you make from your job, a side business, or any other activity is all income. If you sell stocks, bonds, houses, or any other investments for a gain, that's considered income. If you buy a car on Craigslist, keep it for 6 months, and then sell it to somebody else on Craigslist for more than you paid for it and what you put into it for repairs, then that profit is taxable income.

If you trade services with another person and you get the better end of the deal, the monetary equivalent of that gain is also taxable as income. For example, consider a house painter and his neighbor that is an auto mechanic. The house painter agrees to repaint three rooms in his neighbor's home in exchange for a transmission overhaul on his car that would normally cost $1200. If the painter would normally charge $800 to paint those three rooms, then the painter actually got the better end of the deal and must claim the $400 difference as taxable income.

There are plenty of people that obviously ignore this rule, and you may have done it yourself. Some people even do this as a normal course of doing business, especially with the current job market and economic conditions. People that are used to getting paid in cash, just as bartenders, waiters, piano teachers, figure skating coaches, and numerous other professionals, are particularly at risk of falling into this trap.

I cannot emphasize enough the importance of properly reporting all your income, **especially** if you are already on the IRS radar. One of the most common questions that every tax professional is asked has to do with what factors increase your chances of being audited. While it is true that certain deductions and credits claimed on a tax return create a higher risk of being audited, the absolute single biggest risk factor for being audited for a tax return is *already having a tax problem*. If you're reading this book, I can only assume that you fall into this high-risk audit category. Since your audit risk is so much higher than everybody else, it behooves you to report all your income on your tax returns to avoid massive penalties, fines, and perhaps even criminal prosecution for tax evasion.

Remember, the law states that you're required to pay your fair share of tax, and not one penny more. In the world of tax geeks, I consider myself fairly aggressive when it comes to taking deductions and credits, compared to so many tax practitioners that won't enter into anything that looks like a gray area. You should take each and every tax break that you're in any way, shape, or form entitled to. However, you should still report every penny of income, especially if you're already under IRS scrutiny in any way.

Adjustments

Adjustments to income are those things on the first page of a long form 1040 that are directly deducted from your income. These are deductions that everybody can take, even if you don't itemize deductions (Schedule A). Adjustments to income include things like:

- student loan interest
- moving expenses you paid for taking a job somewhere
- half of your self-employment tax
- classroom expenses paid out of pocket by teachers
- alimony you pay
- qualified tuition and related expenses
- contributions to Health Savings Accounts
- contributions to some types of retirement accounts

These deductions come directly off your income, and therefore reduce a very critical number in your income tax calculation: **Adjusted Gross Income** (AGI). AGI is a term we will use frequently. Remember, it's just all your income minus the things listed above. If you paid any of these items, make sure you claim them!

Deductions

Deductions are amounts subtracted from your AGI to determine your taxable income. However, deductions, unlike allowances discussed above, are subject to minimum threshold limits. Since every person is given a "standard deduction", your itemized deductions should exceed this standard deduction in order for you to claim it. In addition, some other deductions have their own minimums before you can claim them. For example, medical expenses have to exceed 10% of your AGI before you can start to claim them.

Here are the most common itemized deductions to be aware of:

- medical and dental expenses that exceed 10% of your AGI
- state and local sales taxes you paid throughout the year
- real estate taxes
- personal property taxes (such as on cars, boats, airplanes, etc.)
- home mortgage interest and points

- mortgage insurance premiums
- interest on investments
- donations to charity
- the value of losses you suffered due to theft or natural disaster

Certain expenses are subject to what is called the 2% floor rule. Like the 10% rule for medical expenses indicated above, the sum of other deduction types has to exceed 2% of your AGI before you can claim them. These expenses include things such as:

- expenses you pay for your job that you are not reimbursed for, such as travel, union dues, uniforms, job-related classes, dry cleaning, etc.
- tax preparation fees
- investments expenses
- safety deposit boxes

Remember, it is the sum total of these types of expenses that have to exceed 2% of your AGI, it is NOT 2% for each individual expense. Also remember that it is the amount in excess of 2% of your AGI that you can deduct.

Don't forget, if you're able to claim any of these deductions, and you think they might add up to more than your standard deduction, then CLAIM THEM. Every deduction reduces your taxable income, and therefore your tax bill.

The standard deduction varies depending on your marital status, and the amounts generally go up every year based on inflation. If you are single or married but filing separate returns, you get the lowest standard deduction ($6,200 for 2014 tax returns). If you are single, but eligible to claim head of household status because you take care of another qualifying person (it does not have to be your own child), then you can claim the next highest standard deduction ($9,100 for 2014). If you are married and filing a joint return, you can claim the highest standard deduction ($12,400 for 2014). If you are blind and either you or yourself exceed the age of 65, you are eligible for special standard deductions.

Your total deductions, whether you take the standard deduction you qualify for or you itemize to get a bigger deduction, is very important. These deductions reduce your taxable income dollar for dollar. As will be discussed later in the chapter on Substitute For Returns, the IRS does not give you anything except the standard deduction for single people if they file a return for you, so you never want them to do this.

Exemptions

While it costs significantly more than $3,950 per year to take care of another person, Congress at least recognizes that it costs *something* to do so. Because of this, you can deduct an additional $3,950 for every other person that you can claim an exemption for. Generally, this includes yourself, your spouse, your own kids that you take care of (even if they don't live with you in some circumstances), other relatives you take care, and in some rare cases, even non-relatives you provide for.

The rules covering whom you can claim as a dependent are a bit complex, and each rule has a list of oddball exceptions. All of those rules are beyond the scope of this book, but Publication 17 has a thorough explanation, and your tax preparer can also help you determine who you can claim and who you can't.

What I would like to emphasize to you regarding dependents is this: If you even think you might be able to claim somebody, at least TRY. You may not think that you can claim an exemption for your kid niece that spent a good chunk of the year with you, but you might actually be surprised. Same with your grandparents in the nursing home. Same with your son's best friend that lived with you all year. Same thing with your kids that lived with your ex all year and you never even saw all year. Most of the rules regarding who can claim who as a dependent come down to the terms of divorce agreements, who spent the money to take care of somebody, how long they lived with you, or who simply has responsibility for the person. Again, try to claim every dependent you can, even if you think you can't – you may just be surprised. You shouldn't claim a dependent that you legally can't, but if by some weird twist of the complex rules you can claim somebody, then do it.

Like adjustments and deductions, exemptions for dependents reduce your taxable income dollar for dollar. The more exemptions you claim, the lower your tax bill is going to be.

Taxable Income and Tax

Your total income from all sources, minus your adjustments, deductions, and exemptions, equals your **taxable income**. Your taxable income is, as the term implies, the amount of your income that is actually subject to tax.

Personal income taxes in the United States are based on marginal tax rates. What this means is that your tax rate is different for different chunks of your taxable income.

For example, a single person's 2014 taxable income is taxed at a rate of 10% on the first $9,075, but at a rate of 15% for any income over $9,075 but less than $36,900. The tax rate jumps again to 25% on income amounts over $36,900 but less than $89,350. This type of tax structure is also called a *progressive* tax, because it keeps increasing with higher income.

Since some part of your income is taxable at one tax rate, and other parts at other tax rates, your overall, combined tax percentage is going to fall somewhere between your highest and lowest marginal tax rates. This is called your **effective tax rate**. Let's take look at a quick example.

John Doe had $20,000 in *taxable income* (after all deductions and exemptions) in 2014, and he is single. The first $9,075 of his income is taxed at 10%, as mentioned above, for a tax of $908 on that first chunk. The rest of his income is taxed at 15%. The remainder comes to $10,925 ($20,000 - $9,075). That $10,925 is taxed at 15%, which comes to $1,639. Adding the two taxes together equals $2,547 in total tax. His tax divided by his taxable income equals 0.12735, or 12.735%. This percentage is John Doe's effective tax rate.

Congress changes the tax rates or the income threshold for each marginal tax rate on an annual basis. It is a large part of the annual political wrangling that goes on in Washington, D.C. between the political parties and different branches of government.

Other Taxes

Besides income taxes, there are other taxes that can be added on to your tax bill on a personal income tax return. The most common example is self-employment tax, which is the equivalent of the Social Security and Medicare taxes that an employer would withhold from your paycheck if you weren't self-employed.

Other taxes that can be added onto your Form 1040 include penalties for early withdrawal of money from retirement accounts, taxes you owe for having household help (such as a maid or nanny), and repayment of certain tax credits, such as the first time home buyer credit from previous years.

Your income tax plus these other taxes are added together to arrive at your total tax.

Tax Credits

Tax credits are important because they have a profound impact on your actual tax bill. Credits don't reduce your taxable income, but rather reduce your tax itself on a dollar for dollar basis. The tax, as calculated above from your taxable income, is some number, which is then reduced $1 for every $1 in tax credits that you are eligible for.

Tax credits are another tool of the political hornet's nest in Congress. Some tax credits are considered “sacred cows” of the system, and much heated debate erupts when a politician suggests changing or eliminating one of them. Other tax credits, such as the home energy efficiency tax credit, are the end result of years of lobbying efforts by special interest groups. Whether you agree or disagree with the political element behind a particular tax credit, the bottom line is that such credits lower your tax bill, and therefore benefit you financially if you are eligible for them.

There are two distinct types of tax credits: Refundable and non-refundable. Most tax credits are non-refundable, meaning that if the sum of these tax credits reduces your tax amount to LESS than zero, you do NOT get the difference back as a refund. Refundable credits, on the other hand, can reduce your tax amount to a negative number and the government will send you a check for the difference as a refund.

The single biggest refundable credit is the Earned Income Credit. This tax credit is the one responsible for giving several thousand dollar refunds to low income individuals that never actually pay a dime in tax. It is one of the “sacred cows” mentioned above to politicians, and is a very controversial tax credit, because it essentially serves as a wealth redistribution mechanism, literally taking money in the form of taxes to people that have higher incomes and giving it to lower income individuals that pay nothing into the system. The Earned Income Credit (EIC) can be as little as a few dollars for somebody with no children, to as much as several thousand dollars for somebody with multiple children and an AGI of less than $20,000. Again, regardless of your political stance on the issue, if you are eligible for this large tax credit, CLAIM IT!

Other tax credits, such as the Child Tax Credit (non-refundable) and the Additional Child Tax Credit (refundable), are directly related to how many eligible children you have. There is also a tax credit for childcare expenses you pay so you can work. If you sent young children to a daycare or had a babysitter or nanny, you may be eligible for this credit.

Other common tax credits we haven't mentioned already include:

- education credits for paying tuition and other fees (non-refundable)
- credit for income tax paid to a foreign government (non-refundable)
- retirement savings contribution credit (non-refundable)
- first time homebuyer credit (refundable)

- Federal fuel tax credit (refundable)
- credits for doing things to stimulate the economy (refundable)
- specially created economic stimulus credits, such as the Making Work Pay credit (refundable)

All of these credits have special rules for eligibility. Again, if you even THINK you may be eligible for one, look into, as every dollar counts. These credits are added up and then subtracted from your total tax, and may be enough to turn a tax bill into a refund.

Refund or Amount You Owe

Everything we've discussed to this point on a tax return boils down to one line: The amount you owe or the amount of your refund. By now, the math should make sense: Your total tax minus your tax credits and minus any payments you made throughout the year (such as income tax withholding from your paycheck or estimated tax payments if you're self-employed) equals some number. If that number is positive, you owe money. If it's negative, you get a refund.

Making sure you claim every adjustment, deduction, exemption, tax credit, and tax payment that you are eligible for is just as important as making sure you claim all your income. The difference, however, is that the IRS simply doesn't care if you don't claim all the deductions and credits you're allowed to – they only care that you claim all your income that you're supposed. YOU need to be the person that cares most about claiming everything that helps you, and you should make sure that your tax preparer, if you use one, also cares deeply about making sure you claim every tax benefit that you can.

Remember, if you owe the IRS money, your penalties and interest are calculated as a direct percentage of what you owe. By claiming every tax benefit you can under the law, you're not just minimizing your tax bill, you're also minimizing the penalties and interest that you have to pay. The end result of missing a few hundred dollars in student loan interest deduction, for example, can actually end up being substantially more than that in extra tax, penalties, and interest.

Bottom line: Don't be shy, claim EVERY tax benefit you're legally entitled to! Give me a call at (818) 889-7285 to schedule a review of your tax returns for potentially missed tax benefits.

Chapter 4: Nasty Things The IRS Can Do To You That You Never Want To Experience

A Notice of Federal Tax Lien (NFTL) is an encumbrance that establishes a legal claim by the government. It does not result in the physical seizure of your property. A levy, on the other hand, allows the IRS to actually seize wages, cash, or property. Levies are normally divided into two categories. The first category includes tangible, real and personal property that you own. The second category includes third parties who hold property belonging to you such as bank deposits and wages.

The first category is often referred to as a "seizure", while the second category is usually referred to as a "levy" or "garnishment". The IRS must file a lien before they can issue a levy and must place a levy upon your property before they can seize your property. Levy action is the usually the most severe collections action the IRS takes against the majority of people that owe back taxes, and it is this type of action that an IRS employee is referring to when they talk about "**enforced collection**."

Federal Tax Liens

Once the IRS makes a valid assessment against you, the IRS is required to give notice and demand for payment within 60 days by law. If you don't pay the taxes owed, a Federal Tax Lien automatically arises and attaches to property and property rights either own directly by you or acquired after the date of the tax assessment. Both Federal law and state law are relevant in determining the effect of the Federal Tax Lien against you and your property. Federal laws determine whether the tax lien has validly attached and state law aids in determining to what property the lien attaches. Under your state laws certain property may be exempt from the lien.

In general, a tax lien gives the IRS a claim against everything you own, from your home and car all the way to the rusted bicycle in your backyard. The lien also technically attaches to your wages, money in you bank accounts, your retirement accounts, and even the cash in your wallet.

A Federal Tax Lien also impacts your credit score, since it shows up on your credit report. Therefore, the tax lien can impact your ability to obtain loans, rent an apartment, and can even impact your insurance rates and ability to obtain employment if you are a job seeker.

In most cases, a tax lien will jump ahead of many other liens against your property after a 180 day period, unless a particular piece of property is used as collateral for a loan. For example, a tax lien does not jump ahead in priority position over a car loan or a first, second, or third mortgage against your home. It will, however, usually jump ahead of, say, a mechanic's lien against your home.

You may have circumstances where having the lien released would be of benefit to helping you resolve the tax situation. There are three types of lien releases available to a taxpayer that may help you resolve tax liabilities with the IRS.

Certificate of Discharge

A Certificate of Discharge (COD) is the process of removing a single piece of property from being subject to the tax lien, usually so that the property can be legally transferred. For example, if you are trying to sell your house but the presence of the lien is preventing this from occurring, then you would need to obtain a Certificate of Discharge to release the tax lien against your house.

In the vast majority of cases, the IRS will not release a lien against a particular piece of property unless they are somehow going to benefit from it. They will generally approve a Certificate of Discharge if the lien discharge will facilitate the sale of the property in such a way that the IRS will get some money out of it. In other words, releasing the lien will facilitate collection of the tax.

If the government isn't going to see any money out of releasing a piece of property from the lien, it's possible to still obtain a Certificate of Discharge if there is a valid reason. In particular, if the IRS won't be receiving any money, but getting rid of the property will free up cash flow and put you in a better financial position in regards to your income and expenses so that later on down the road you can start paying on your taxes, then the IRS will likely approve a Certificate of Discharge.

If the property in question has no significant fair market value, the COD may also be granted, but this is much more of a hit-or-miss situation.

Lien Subordination

A lien subordination is the process of moving the tax lien down a notch in the prioritization of claims against a piece of property. For example, if you own a house free and clear, and the tax lien is in first position against the house, you can't obtain a mortgage against the house. No lender in their right mind is going to loan you money against that house unless their lien is going to take first position.

The answer to this problem is the lien subordination.

The IRS will usually approve the subordination of their lien against a property if the lien that will be taking first position ahead of the tax lien will result in money going to your tax liability.

In the house example, obtaining a subordination of the tax lien in order to obtain a mortgage against the house will result in cash coming from that mortgage. At closing, that cash will go directly to the IRS, the mortgage will move into first position, and the tax lien gets re-recorded in second position.

Remember, paying interest on a loan is almost always going to be cheaper than paying penalties and interest to the IRS.

There are other conditions where a lien subordination will still be approved, even if the IRS isn't going to obtain direct proceeds from doing so. For example, many trucking companies will finance their accounts receivable through a process called factoring. In factoring, a lender pays the trucking company some percentage of their accounts receivable (usually 75% to 90%) up front, and then the lender takes the responsibility of collecting on that account receivable when it's due, usually 30 to 90 days down the road. This way, the trucking company gets money now so that they can buy fuel and make payroll.

When a tax lien is filed, most factoring lenders stop funding. In that case, the trucking company suddenly loses all it's cash flow. In order to enable the funding to continue, a lien subordination can be obtained that move the tax lien to a position below the factoring lender, thereby protecting the lender's claim on those accounts receivable.

Lien Withdrawal

There are rare occasions when obtaining an outright release of the entire Federal tax lien is actually the best way to progress towards a resolution of your tax liabilities. If a case can be made that the withdrawal of the lien will facilitate payment of the tax liability, or is otherwise in the best interest of both the taxpayer and the government, then the government may be open to this.

Another case where a lien withdrawal can be applied for is when you have entered into an Installment Agreement to pay the back taxes and the agreement did not mandate that a lien be filed, particularly a payment plan where the payments are directly withdrawn from your bank account. In these cases, you can often get the lien released as long as you are current with your payments and other tax obligations.

Certificate of Release of Paid or Unenforceable Lien

The IRS is required to issue a certificate of release of lien no later than 30 days after one of the following events occur:

- The tax liability is paid in full.
- The tax liability is no longer collectible. In other words, the 10-year statute of limitations on collections has expired.
- The IRS accepts the bond of a surety company or payment of all taxes owed is to be made no later than six months before the expiration of the 10-year collection statute.
- The taxpayer delivers a cashier's check to the IRS and receives a Certificate of Release of Tax Lien.

Bank Account Levies

An IRS levy is the actual action taken by the IRS to collect past due taxes. For example, the IRS can issue a bank levy to obtain your cash in savings and checking accounts or the IRS can levy your wages or accounts receivable, if you run a business.

The person, company or institution that is served the levy must comply or face their own IRS problems. For example, when the IRS issues a levy against your bank accounts, your bank must comply. The bank is required to take the funds out of your account to which the levy attaches on the day they process the levy. They must then hold those funds for 21 days and then after the 21 days, send those funds to the IRS. If they fail to do this, the IRS will come after your bank and penalize them. The additional paperwork that the bank or other company or institution is faced with to comply with the levy usually causes your relationship to suffer with the person or institution being levied.

When a financial institution receives a levy on your bank account, it cannot surrender the money until 21 calendar days after the levy has been served. This 21-day waiting period provides you the opportunity to notify the IRS and correct any errors regarding your accounts. An extension of this 21-day period may be granted by the Area Director of the IRS if there is a legitimate dispute regarding the amount of tax owed. Anytime during the 21-day waiting period the levy can be released. During these 21 days it is imperative that you exercise your appeals rights. In this case, you will want to file a CAP appeal. CAP stands for Collection Appeals Process. When you file a CAP appeal, the IRS must hear your case within five days. Please see the chapter on Appeals for more information about this process.

Levies should be avoided at all costs and are usually the result of poor communication with your Revenue Officer. When the IRS levies a bank account, the levy is only for the particular day the levy is received by the bank. As I mentioned, the bank is required to remove whatever amount of money is available in your account that day up to the maximum amount of the IRS levy and send it to the IRS after that 21 day hold period. This type of levy does not affect future deposits. So if your bank account gets levied today and all the money is taken out by the bank to be sent to the IRS 21 days later, you can make a deposit tomorrow that is not subject to that IRS levy.

An IRS wage levy is quite different. Wage levies are filed with your employer and remain in effect until the IRS notifies the employer that the wage levy has been released. Most wage levies take so much money from your paycheck that you don't have enough money to live on. In most circumstances, an IRS wage garnishment will take 70% to 80% of your entire paycheck. For most taxpayers, wage garnishments are the worst thing the IRS can do to them, and everything possible should be done to avoid this debilitating attack on your personal finances.

Personal Property Levies

The IRS's levy power is extremely broad and does not require that the IRS take you to court. The IRS can use its authority to gain possession of your property to pay any back taxes owed and all they have to do is file a notice in demand of payment, wait 10 days, then file a 30-day notice of intent to levy. After that 30 days, they can then levy. The effect of a levy is to compel you to turn property over to the IRS. Amounts that the IRS gains from a levy or garnishment are applied to your tax debt as follows:

1. The proceeds are applied to the expenses of the levy in sale.

2. Proceeds from the levy are then applied to the tax specifically relating to the levied property.

3. Proceeds are then applied to the delinquent tax liability that caused the whole situation in the first place.

4. Funds collected by a levy are considered to have been paid involuntarily. Therefore, you cannot specify to the IRS how you want those funds applied, which you are normally able to do if you make voluntary payments. This is yet another reason why levies are best avoided.

As we already mentioned, the IRS is required to notify you of its intent to levy you at least 30 days before the levy. This is done thru a notice called a Letter 1058 and states across the top of the notice, "Final Notice of Intent to Levy". When you are issued a Letter 1058 by the IRS, you have broad appeals right that allows you to appeal the proposed action. However, your appeal must be submitted within the 30 day window. If you've recently receive a final notice of intent to levy, please see the Chapter on Appeals to learn how to file a Collection Due Process appeal.

Seizures

The IRS must issue a notice of seizure to the owner of any real property (e.g. real estate) or the possessor of personal property as soon as practicable after the property is seized. This notice has the same effect as the Notice of Levy and can be delivered in person to the owner or possessor of the property or left at your home or normal place of business. Seizures must always be approved by upper IRS management. The supervisor must review your information, verify that the balance is due and affirm that a lien, levy or seizure is appropriate under the circumstances. Failure to give the proper notice will invalidate the seizure and afford you certain legal rights.

Seizures of your residence or business

The IRS is no longer really in the business of seizing homes and entire businesses. These sorts of seizures have become relatively infrequent, largely in due to the adverse publicity that the IRS has received from conducting these actions. The Taxpayer Bill of Rights prohibits the IRS from seizing real property that is used as a residence by the taxpayer for tax amounts of $5,000 or less, including penalties and interest. The Taxpayer Bill of Rights also only permits a levy or seizure on a principal residence if a judge approves of the seizure in writing. Following the 1998 Restructuring Amendments to the Internal Revenue Code, the process for seizing your home has become incredibly difficult for the IRS, which is a good thing for you.

Wage Garnishments

The IRS wage garnishment is a very powerful tool used to collect taxes owed by bringing your employer into the situation. A wage garnishment cannot only be an inconvenience and an embarrassment but it can also leave you with no money to pay your regular living expenses. Once a wage garnishment is filed with your employer, the employer is required to collect the vast majority of each of your paychecks and send that money to the IRS. As mentioned earlier, the wage garnishment will usually take 70% to 80% of your paycheck. In addition, if you receive Social Security, the IRS can take up to 15% of each and every one of your Social Security checks. The wage garnishment stays in effect until either the IRS is paid or the IRS agrees to release the garnishment.

A wage garnishment can be appealed through the Collection Appeals Program, just like a bank account levy. In addition, wage garnishments are a situation where seeking assistance from the Taxpayer Advocate can be extremely helpful.

Fair Debt Collection Practices Act

The IRS is subject to the conditions of the Fair Debt Collection Practices Act just like any other debt collector. This Act includes a number of rules controlling debt collection practices. Normally, these rules are to prevent excessive collections practices from being undertaken by collection agencies for things such as credit card debts and automobile payments. However, the Taxpayer Bill of Rights follows the Fair Debt Collection Practices Act guidelines and provides you certain rights.

For example, you cannot be contacted by a Collections Representative of the IRS outside of the hours of 8AM to 9PM, and it also prohibits harassing or abusive behavior from the IRS to you. The IRS may not communicate with you at an unusual time or place which is known or which should be known to be inconvenient to you. The IRS can also not communicate with you regarding your tax liability at your place of employment if the IRS knows or has reason to know that the your employer prohibits you from receiving such communication.

If the IRS knows that you are represented by someone who is authorized to practice before the IRS, then they can also not contact you. This provision does not apply if your power of attorney representative does not respond to the IRS within a reasonable period of time after being requested to do so. That is why it's important that if you hire professional tax resolution representation that you hire a reputable firm that's going to actually do what you pay them to do.

Chapter 5: Of Time & Taxes

Statutes of limitations in regards to tax matters are important for you to understand because the different statutes of limitations give you different rights and responsibilities in regards to the tax matters involved. There are some statutes of limitations that work for you and there are others that can obviously work against you. It is important for you to understand these statutes of limitations when dealing with the Internal Revenue Service so that you aren't chasing a ghost or trying to make a case that can't be made.

From the government's perspective, the statute of limitations restricts your rights in many ways, such as the restriction on claiming a refund of tax you overpaid or limiting initial actions to obtain refunds.

Now, a statute of limitations may also restrict what the IRS can do against you. The statute of limitations restricts them from collecting a deficiency in tax after a certain amount of time, and also prevents the IRS from asserting either civil or criminal cases.

Either way you look at it, the statute of limitations issue provides a date of finality after which actions may not be taken by either the IRS or by you which is why it is essential for you to understand them.

Let's first look at the three-year rules. First, the IRS must assess a tax within three years after the date that you file a tax return. This three-year period also applies to penalties. Now, when is a tax return considered filed for the purposes of this rule? A return is treated as being filed on time even if it's received by the IRS after the return's due date.

Timely filing is determined by the postmark stamped on the envelope by the U.S. Postal Service or by a private delivery service. That is why whenever you send a tax return or other important items such as an Installment Agreement proposal or an Offer in Compromise application, or an Appeal, I highly recommend that you always send it by certified mail with return receipt requested.

There does not appear to be a "bright line" test to determine whether a tax return lacking a required form is a valid return. Courts will typically apply the "substantial compliance standard" to the facts of each case. This means that there must be adequate information on the return to calculate the tax liability even if a required form was omitted. The document must also indicate that it is, in fact, a tax return. An honest and reasonable attempt must be made to satisfy the tax law and you must execute the return under penalties of perjury, which is what you're doing whenever you sign the bottom of a tax return. Next time you have a tax return in front of you, take a look at what you're actually signing.

A complete tax return that lacks a specific required form such as a schedule or attachment is still sufficient to begin the statute of limitations running for assessment purposes. So for example, if you file your 1040 personal income tax return but you forget to include a Schedule E. Your income from that Schedule E is on the front page of the Form 1040. The IRS can't say that you didn't file a timely return and therefore they have to start the clock ticking on the statute of limitations for the assessment of the tax as soon as they get it.

There are special statute of limitations rules that you need to be aware of as well. When the IRS produces a Substitute for Return – which is prepared by the IRS when you don't file the tax return – this does not start running the statute of limitations for assessment. In order to start the clock running on the 3-year assessment statute of limitations, you have to file a proper tax return yourself. So, if you have been notified by the IRS that they prepared the return on your behalf, it is generally advisable to file a n actual, original return as soon as possible.

A six-year statute of limitations, instead of three years,

applies to returns that omit a substantial amount of income. "Substantial" means an amount of income which exceeds 25% of the gross income reported on the original tax return. The limitations period is extended to the tax payer's entire tax liability for that year, not just the omitted items.

This applies only to innocent or negligent omissions of gross income. The six-year limitations period does not apply to fraudulent omissions of gross income. If you fraudulently omit reporting income on a tax return, the tax may be assessed at any time.

Here's a bonus tip for you: The burden of proof rests with the IRS in proving that the 25% omission from income did in fact occur. The IRS cannot solely rely on the amount of unreported income asserted in the Notice of Deficiency they mail you, which they're required to send you by law

The Internal Revenue Code states that the IRS can assess tax or bring a suit to collect an unassessed tax at any time regardless of any statute of limitations for some specific situations. Here are those situations:

1. You fail to file the tax return.
2. A false or fraudulent return is filed with the intent to evade the tax.

3. The tax payer attempts to defeat or evade the tax.

4. Once the tax payer files a fraudulent return, the tax payer cannot later start the running of the three-year statute of limitations period by filing an amended return to include the omitted income.

Next, let's talk about statute of limitations on collection of a tax. Once the IRS has assessed the tax within the assessment statute of limitations as discussed above, the IRS then has 10 years in which to collect the tax. There are certain events that can extend the statutory period past the 10-year mark, because they actually "stop the clock". These events include:

- filing bankruptcy
- filing certain appeal requests
- entering into litigation with the IRS
- filing an Offer in Compromise
- filing a request for an Installment Agreement
- requesting a military deferment

- filing an innocent spouse defense

With these actions, the statute of limitations is temporarily suspended while that action is being investigated.

The date of assessment is the date the Assessment Officer signs the Summary Record of Assessment. This information can be verified by obtaining an IRS account transcript called a Record of Account, which you can request from the IRS at any time. If the Summary Record of Assessment was not properly recorded, then the assessment is actually not proper. Some penalties have a different assessment date from that of the original tax. In those cases the penalty has a separate Collection Statute Expiration Date (CSED), which is the date that the 10-year period ends.

The IRS can use administrative or judicial methods to collect delinquent taxes. The IRS generally precedes administratively by levying and seizing assets that you own. If the IRS embarks upon this course of action, the levy must occur within the 10-year statute of limitations period. The IRS can also precede judicially by filing a lawsuit against you within the 10-year limitation period.

During a period of time in which an Installment Agreement request is pending with the IRS, the statute of limitations on collections is suspended for a while.

The period is 30 days following a rejection of a proposed Installment Agreement or 30 days following the termination of an Installment Agreement. The statute of limitations on collections is also suspended during an Offer in Compromise investigation. During the time that the IRS is considering your Offer in Compromise, the statute of limitations clock isn't running. It is also not running for the 30 days following the rejection of an Offer in Compromise.

The situation is similar for bankruptcy. A bankruptcy petition prohibits the IRS from assessing or collecting a claim from you which arose prior to the bankruptcy petition being filed. During this period the assessment limitations period – the three- and six-year period as discussed earlier – is suspended, plus a period of 60 days after the discharge of your bankruptcy. The limitation period for collection is suspended during your bankruptcy petition period and for an additional six months after the bankruptcy is discharged.

There are times where an Appeals Officer is involved in your case. The settlement authority of an Appeals Officer is very broad. However, their primary job is to resolve the tax issue expeditiously and to weigh the costs of potential litigation for the IRS.

The appeals process is one where professional negotiation skills can really come in handy. Since the appeals process relies so much upon negotiation, a high percentage of cases are resolved here. It is not uncommon for those of us that are professional tax resolution representatives to simply resolve our clients' cases in the appeals process rather than relying on a field Revenue Officer to work with us.

The biggest thing that you need to remember is that the first step in the collection process is for the IRS to actually assess the tax. Until this occurs, the IRS cannot act to collect on that tax. An assessment is simply what the IRS claims you owe. The most common forms of assessment are summary assessments and deficiency assessments.

Summary assessment will usually represent the amount reflected on a tax return that you filed, whereas a deficiency assessment can occur due to an adjustment being made to a filed tax return, such as the result of an audit, or when the IRS files a Substitute for Return.

Chapter 6: Understanding IRS Collections And The Resolution Process

The U.S. Internal Revenue Service is the single largest collections agency in the world. In 2010, the IRS spent over $12.5 billion and employed just under 95,000 people to collect more than $2.3 trillion in tax revenue. Of these 95,000 personnel, over 20,000 are directly involved in enforced collections action against taxpayers that owe back taxes.

Needless to say, this is a bill collector that can have a serious impact on your life, especially given the collections actions they can take that other bill collectors can't.

It is important to understand that the IRS is a slow moving bureaucracy that is highly resistant to change, and is heavily driven by forms and written procedures. This doesn't bode well when it comes to fixing your tax problem quickly, but it does provide a major benefit to working to resolve your tax problem: Their playbook is public record, and they're required to follow it.

Here in this chapter, I'm going to provide you an overview of the flow of the IRS collections process and the tax resolution process. Both processes have a very logical, linear flow. In the chapters that follow, we will discuss specific aspects of the tax resolution process, so that you can jump to the chapter and section that is specifically applicable to you, based on where you are in the linear flow of IRS collections.

Collections Starts With A Tax Deficiency

The IRS doesn't start collections activity against you simply because you file a tax return with a balance due and don't pay it. In fact, the collections process really doesn't even start when the tax assessment is made.

In all reality, the IRS collections process begins with a letter called the Statutory Notice of Deficiency (SNOD). Within the industry, we also refer to this as the "21 day letter". This letter is kicked out by a computer automatically when your "number comes up". This can actually be substantially after your tax return was filed. For individuals that file their tax return on time (by April 15th), it's not uncommon to get the SNOD two to four months after the end of tax season. For business that are behind on payroll taxes, I've seen cases where it take an entire year before the IRS kicks out the SNOD. This delay has been one of the primary things reported by the Taxpayer Advocate to Congress as a major problem within the IRS.

The SNOD is referred to as the 21-day letter because it gives you 21 days in which to pay the tax before additional penalties and interest will accrue on the tax liability. Nothing "bad" is going to happen to you during this period.

Notice of Federal Tax Lien Filing (Form 668-Y)

If you fail to pay your tax bill during the 21-day period of the SNOD, don't set up a payment plan, and don't contest the validity of the tax bill, then the next automatic step, again performed by a computer, is the filing of a Notice of Federal Tax Lien (NFTL). Under new rules issued in February 2011, the IRS will only file an actual tax lien against you if your total tax debt exceeds $10,000, including any prior years you may owe for.

As discussed earlier, a tax lien attaches to everything you own, including your wages and all your property. In addition, a tax lien is eventually indicated on your credit report, and can impact you in numerous ways, also discussed in the earlier chapter on tax liens.

Notice of Intent to Levy (Form Letter CP-504)

Approximately 30 to 45 days after the filing of an actual tax lien, a computer will again kick out another notice to you. This notice will be titled "Notice of Intent to Levy" and contain a designation in the upper right or lower right corner labeled “CP-504”.

When you receive a CP-504, it is important to know one major thing: It has no teeth. It is a letter required to be sent to you by law, to notify you that, because of the tax lien, the IRS has the authority to take serious collections action against, such as levies. In reality, the letter itself doesn't grant any rights to either you or the IRS, but when you receive it, it's important to mark it on the calendar, because 30 days after the CP-504, you're going to get something much, much more important.

Final Notice of Intent to Levy (Letter 1058)

Exactly 30 days after a CP-504 is issued, you're going to get another form letter from the IRS, labeled “Final Notice of Intent to Levy”. In the upper right or lower right corner will be “Letter 1058”.

Letter 1058 is important for two reasons:

1. It is the first opportunity you have to file an Appeal.

2. Thirty days after this letter, the IRS can actually levy you.

Here's the bottom line thing to understand about the Letter 1058: If you don't file an Appeal of this notice, the IRS *can* initiate levy action 30 days after they send this notice. In other words, you can safely ignore a lien and a CP-504, but you simply can't ignore a Letter 1058.

Does a Letter 1058 mean that the IRS *will* levy you? No, it doesn't, particularly if they don't have the information necessary to issue a levy. For example, if they don't know where you bank and don't know where you work, they can't very well issue a levy. However, if you still work at the same job that you had when you filed the tax return, the IRS knows where you work, because they received a copy of your W-2 from your employer. Also, if you have in the past given the IRS your bank account number and bank routing number in order to have a refund direct deposited, then they know where your bank is.

Whenever you receive a Letter 1058, you should file an Appeal. In order to do this, file Form 12153, *Request for Collection Due Process Appeal*. Further information about filing this appeal, called a “CDP” for short, is available in the Appeals chapter, later in this book. Normally, in my practice I will file a CDP appeal about 20 days into the 30 day window for doing so, in order to give my client as much time as possible to get their finances in order.

The Cycle Repeats

The cycle of SNOD → NFTL → CP-504 → Letter 1058 repeats itself any time you incur a new tax liability. For individual taxpayers, that means this cycle could repeat itself once per year. For a business dealing with employment taxes, this cycle could basically never end, since payroll tax returns are filed quarterly, and this cycle takes about 4 months to complete.

Revenue Officer Assignment

Your first time through this cycle, your case will exist within a division of the IRS called the Automated Collection System (ACS). ACS personnel are located at several of the largest IRS service centers, including Ogden, UT, Cincinnati, OH, and Philadelphia, PA. The majority of letters you receive from the IRS will be from one of these service centers.

Unless your collections case has special circumstances associated with it, you will usually stay assigned to ACS even if you accumulate two or three year's worth of tax debt as an individual, or 3 or 4 quarters of payroll tax liability for a business. After reaching this threshold, your case will likely be assigned to a

Revenue Officer. Revenue Officers (RO) are field agents that live and work in local community all over the United States. There are currently over 14,000 of these personnel working for the IRS.

An interesting thing about the current economic situation is that there are a growing number of taxpayers falling into trouble with the IRS. Because of this, the waiting line for assignment to an RO is many areas of the country is growing longer and longer. Certain taxpayers are bumped ahead of the line, depending on their circumstances. But for most taxpayers, they are waiting longer and longer, which gives them more and more time to get their finances in order and hopefully be able to work out something once they *do* get assigned to a field agent.

I've mentioned several times that there are certain circumstances that will get you assigned to a Revenue Officer much faster. Some of those circumstances include:

- your total tax debt is particularly large
- your tax liability for a particular year is quite large
- you've accumulated personal tax debt for three or more years

- you have more than 4 quarters of payroll tax liability and continue to accrue more
- you owe taxes and are not actively making Federal Tax Deposits (payroll taxes) or Estimated Tax Payments (if you're self-employed)

When you are assigned to a Revenue Officer, the course of your tax case takes a sudden shift. Having an experienced, trained human being looking at your tax case, and passing judgement on you based on what's in a file and thereby determining how they are going to handle your tax case, means a lot.

The Tax Resolution Process

Whether your case is still assigned to ACS, or if it's been assigned to a Revenue Officer, there is a fairly standard, step-by-step process by which your tax case gets resolved. Since the IRS has their own procedures that employees have to follow, you can always know what the next action from the IRS Collections division is going to be.

In general, these are the steps that you will need to follow to make progress towards a successful and permanent tax resolution:

1. Contact ACS or your Revenue Officer and negotiate a time period of 30 to 120 days in order to get your affairs in order for resolving your tax situation.

2. File appeals on any items which you are eligible to do so.

3. File all past due tax returns, including replacing SFR's.

4. Complete a Collection Information Statement, including supporting documentation, to determine your current financial condition.

5. Determine the best resolution strategy based on your financial condition.

6. Apply for and negotiate towards the chosen resolution strategy.

7. Go through the Appeals process, if necessary.

8. Apply for a penalty abatement, if necessary.

These are the same big picture steps that I follow myself when working with a client.

Chapter 7: Offer In Compromise Program

Whenever you hear the phrase "pennies on the dollar" in relation to tax resolution, you are hearing a reference to the Offer in Compromise (OIC) program.

The OIC program is intended to give taxpayer's without the financial means to pay their tax debt to pay whatever they have, and then start over. In many ways, an OIC is akin to a bankruptcy filing on taxes only. The major difference, however, is that an OIC is an administrative proceeding, rather than a court proceeding.

An Offer in Compromise application will require complete financial disclosure. In other words, a full and accurate Form 433-A or Form 433-B will be required, along with *complete* supporting documentation. Because the government is going to accept less money for the tax debt than what you owe, they are going to go to great lengths to make sure that you actually qualify.

You should note that almost 80% of all Offers in Compromise are ultimately rejected by the IRS, either via the Offer process itself, or in Appeals. The biggest reason that Offers are rejected is because the applicant simply wasn't eligible for the program.

Some taxpayers file an OIC simply to "buy time" to

figure something else out, since the process normally takes 6 to 9 months for an Offer application to be processed and denied, including Appeals. While this may be a worthwhile strategy for you, you should note the CSED is extended day-for-day while your Offer is in process, and for 30 days after it is ultimately denied.

Eligibility

Your eligibility to settle for less than what you owe is directly related to your offer amount (see "Offer Calculation"). If your offer amount is equal to or greater than the minimum amount calculated using the IRS formula, then you may be eligible to file an Offer in Compromise.

Like other resolution options, the IRS also requires that you:

- have filed all past due tax returns
- are not currently generating new tax liabilities
- agree to properly file and pay on all tax returns, on time, for the next 5 years
- agree to let the IRS keep any tax refunds you would otherwise be due during the time you are paying on the OIC

Failure to abide by these rules will either result in

rejection of your offer, or default of your offer agreement and reinstatement of any tax liabilities that were eliminated.

Payment Options

In addition to a $150 application fee, you are required to make payments on the Offer in Compromise unless you meet low income qualification guidelines for an exception to this rule.

The first payment option is used when you will pay the entire amount of your settlement offer in 5 monthly payments or less. If you use this option, you may pay the entire offer amount when submitting your application, or include a minimum 20% deposit (non-refundable!) and take up to a maximum of 5 more monthly payments to pay off your offer. Using this payment option provides the benefit of not being required to make regular payments on your Offer while it is being processed. Using this option also generally results in paying the smallest possible Offer amount.

The second payment option requires you to make regular payments on your Offer in Compromise while the IRS is considering it. These payments are non-refundable, and the first payment needs to be included with your offer application. The second payment option takes longer than 5 months to pay off. Under the new

OIC rules, you can essentially take as long as you want to make these payments.

Older OIC guidelines had three payment options: The 5-month option now called Payment Option 1 (formerly called "Lump Sum Cash Offer"), another option with a 24 month payment limit (formerly called the "Short Term Periodic Payment Offer"), and a third option allowing up to 60 months or until your CSED, whichever was longer. The new payment options get rid of the confusing names and combine two longer old options.

Regardless of the payment option you use, your payments must add up to the total offer amount, and your offer amount must be at least your Reasonable Collection Potential (RCP), discussed next.

Keep in mind that penalties and interest continue to build on your tax liability while you make Offer payments, even though ultimately those penalties and interest go away when the Offer is paid off and settled. If you default on your OIC, however, those built up penalties and interested are added back on to your balance and you will be liable for it.

Offer Calculation

Many unlicensed tax resolution salespeople, either through ignorance or simply gross incompetence, will tell everybody that they talk to that they qualify for an OIC, and that the Offer amount is some percentage of what they owe.

In addition to this horrifically unethical practice, many tax resolution firms will also only tout their most successful OIC applications, showing you that they did indeed get 1.2 cents on the dollar for one client, and 4 cents on the dollar for another client, all while failing to inform you that:

a. Most of their OIC applications for clients were outright rejected, and

b. of those that were accepted, it was usually only for 50 or 75 cents on the dollar.

The Offer amount is the single most important part of a successful OIC application. Calculating the OIC offer amount is extremely formulaic, and requires a complete and accurate Form 433 to be filled out. The IRS goes through an extensive investigation phase to verify information on your Form 433, looking for other assets you own and income you failed to disclose. The IRS looks at various public records sources, and may even pull a credit report to verify what you've told them (this action doesn't require your direct authorization to the

IRS under Federal law).

Within the IRS booklet containing the OIC application, there are versions of the Form 433-A and Form 433-B that are modified slightly for OIC purposes. If you use the PDF version of the booklet (search for "IRS Form 656B"), the calculations are actually carried forward for you to the lines that determine your Offer amount.

The entire purpose of these calculations is to arrive at what the IRS calls your "Reasonable Collection Potential", or RCP. The RCP is the sum of the net worth of your assets plus all of your disposable income for the next 4 or 5 years. In other words:

Settlement Amount = (monthly disposable income x a number of months) + the net realizable equity in the taxpayer's assets)

Disposable income is monthly income minus allowable monthly expenses. It is important to recognize that the IRS will not allow all expenses that you may actually have. Common disallowed expenses are college tuition payments for a dependent and credit card payments (disallowed since they represent unsecured debt). For more information on this topic, refer to the chapter on IRS Collection Information Statements.

The number of months over which disposable income must be calculated into the offer amount is based on the smaller of the number of months remaining until the

Collection Statute Expiration Date (CSED) for the tax debt OR either 48 or 60 months, depending on the payment option for the OIC which the applicant is selecting.

"Net realizable equity in assets" is the quick sale value of the asset (often 80% of Fair Market Value (FMV)) minus any liabilities which are secured by the asset (e.g., a loan). As an example, if a taxpayer has a home worth $100,000 and owes $50,000 on the home, the IRS will calculate the net realizable equity in the asset as follows: ($100,000 x .80) - $50,000 = $30,000. The IRS expects, in this example, that the $30,000 will be included in the Offer amount.

Based on this explanation of how RCP is determined, and understanding that RCP is your minimum offer amount, I hope it is apparent as to why the IRS rejects so many OIC applications. In reality, the best OIC candidates are folks that have very little in the way of assets, and no disposable income. The best OIC candidates often tend to be unemployed and broke.

Application Process – What To Expect

When you file an OIC, a Process Examiner will look over your paperwork to make sure that the offer is "processable", meaning that you met all the administrative requirements to be eligible, properly filled out the forms, crossed your t's and dotted your i's, filled out a complete Form 433, and have filed all your tax returns.

If your Offer is deemed to be not processable, it will be returned to you with a letter from the Process Examiner explaining what you need to correct, and to resubmit your offer with those corrections.

If considered processable, an Offer Examiner will then be assigned to actually review the merits and financial aspects of your application. This is the person that verifies assets, orders credit reports, and basically gets very up close and personal regarding every aspect of your financial situation or the financial health of your business.

The Offer Examiner will usually provide you the opportunity to address any inconsistencies they discover in their findings, and to argue on your own behalf for the inclusion or exclusion of certain assets or expenses. More often than not, this is the phase where having a professional representative comes in handy the most, to handle these negotiations for you.

Once the Offer Examiner has all the information they need to either accept or reject your Offer, they will do so, and send you a letter explaining why.

Keep in mind that for Payment Option 2, you must continue to make monthly payments on your OIC while this review process is going on.

If you fail to do so, your offer will automatically be rejected, and the IRS will keep the money you did pay and apply it to your tax liability as they see fit.

Appeals

If your OIC is rejected, you have the right to know why, and also the right to Appeal this decision. More often than not, a dispute over including an asset or expense item will be the argument you take to Appeals. Appeals Officers have the authority to accept or reject an OIC based on their own findings, rather than the findings of the Offer Examiner.

Chapter 8: Reducing IRS Penalties With Reasonable Cause Penalty Abatements

There are a lot of common misconceptions surrounding the abatement (removal) of IRS penalties and interest.

First of all, it is important for anybody that owes the IRS money to understand that you will not have interest charges removed. If somebody is trying to sell you on their tax relief services and they tell you that they can have the amount of interest on your tax account reduced or eliminated, they're lying. The provisions within the U.S. tax code for eliminating interest charges on back taxes are extremely limited and extremely specific, and if you owe the money but just simply couldn't or didn't pay it, you DO NOT qualify.

The second thing to understand is that the removal of any penalties is extremely formulaic. You must meet one of the reasonable cause criteria outlined by the Internal Revenue Code. Fortunately, these reasonable cause criteria are much broader and more applicable to more people and businesses than are the criteria for interest abatement. Some of the possible reasonable cause criteria include death or illness in the family, loss of records, and receiving bad advice from a CPA.

It is important to note that the two most common causes

for accrual of a tax liability are not considered reasonable cause by the IRS, and most often you will not be able to have penalties reduced for these two reasons. These reasons are:

1. Ignorance of filing or deposit requirements
2. Cash flow problems that leave you without enough money to pay the tax when due

Under special circumstances, the IRS will grant penalty relief due to economic hardship, but it is a hard case to prove and tends to be a longer, more drawn out process through the Appeals division. The granting of this sort of penalty relief can also depend upon which Circuit Court of Appeals district you live in, since different case law has been interpreted in a different court jurisdictions.

Above all, just remember that you can get penalties abated, if you have a good reason that was beyond your control and that can be backed up with proper documentation. And as far as interest charges go – forget about it, the IRS is not going to let you off the hook for those if you actually do owe the tax.

One of the biggest things I am adamant about is correcting the myths, lies, and half-truths perpetuated by unlicensed tax resolution salespeople, and the IRS penalty abatement is one of the things least understood and grossly over-hyped by salespeople in our industry.

The "we can remove interest charges" lie, as mentioned at the start of this chapter, is one of the biggest lies that tax resolution sales people tell their propsects.

There are two, and precisely two, instances in which interest is reduced:

1. An IRS employee gives you false information, which you acted on and resulted in the interest. This is one reason why all IRS correspondence should be conducted and followed up in writing.

2. Since interest is calculated based on the tax liability, if an amended return is filed and the tax itself is lowered, then the interest is also reduced.

Reasonable Cause Criteria

Now, on to penalties. The IRS charges dozens of different types of penalties, but the three that we most commonly talk about are the late filing penalty, the late payment penalty, and the penalty for not making Federal Tax Deposits. These three penalties combined can add a whopping 65% to your total IRS bill. If your tax debt is more than two years old, you've maxed out all these penalties, and therefore over half your total debt is penalties.

The IRS does actually have a compassionate side, and it's generally found in the penalty abatement process. Penalty abatement applications can also be appealed if initially denied, so you can always get a second set of eyeballs on the issue. The thing to keep in mind is that the IRS has very strict guidelines for granting penalty abatements, and these guidelines are referred to as "reasonable cause criteria".

As mentioned earlier, "we didn't have the money" is NOT a reasonable cause criteria. A drop in revenue, by itself, is insufficient argument for obtaining penalty relief. Any request for penalty abatement simply citing the economic recession will be immediately denied.

Why is this? Here is the IRS' logic: You made the money, and should have paid the taxes at the time on that money. If you are self-employed and receive a check, then you HAD the money, you simply didn't give the IRS their chunk of it. Same goes with payroll taxes for businesses, particularly the trust fund taxes (money you withhold from employee paychecks for income tax and Medicare/Social Security): If you had the expectation to pay some amount of wage, then you theoretically HAD the money sitting somewhere to pay that person, and should have withheld it and turned it over to the IRS. If you couldn't cover the taxes, you shouldn't have had the employee and should have laid people off or cut back their hours.

There are ways to argue around this, and we have done so very successfully, but there has to be some other circumstance. For example, you had the money to pay the tax, but paying the tax instead of something else would have created an "undue hardship".

Examples of "undue hardship" could include a large medical expense that unpaid would have left a condition untreated, or a court ordered payment that, if missed, would have resulted in other legal consequences, or a bill such as a large automobile repair which would have left you unable to get to work and resulted in job loss.

These arguments are difficult to make and require significantly more work than standard reasonable cause criteria applications, but they CAN be won, especially in the Appeals process.

The primary IRS penalty abatement reasonable cause criteria center around natural disasters, loss or destruction of vital business records, bad advice from the IRS or an accounting professional, criminal activity, medical issues, substance abuse problems, and other serious circumstances.

A couple years ago I developed a standard list of questions to ask clients to assist me in preparing their penalty abatement. This list of questions should be given some serious thought before requesting penalty abatement, as you are more likely to get what you want if your request covers one of these areas:

- Were any financial records lost or destroyed?
- Was there any transition in your business that lead to the failure to pay taxes, such as a change of ownership?
- Was there a death or serious illness that directly affected your ability to work or impacted the operation of your business?
- Were you the victim of any embezzlement of funds, theft of valuable property, or identity theft?
- Were there any alcohol or drug abuse issues that affected your business or your personal wage earning capability?
- Was there a natural disaster that impacted you or your business?
- Did you rely on the advice of a CPA or IRS employee in making tax decisions?
- Were there any circumstances that created substantial financial hardship, to the point where

either yourself or your business was close to going bankrupt?

These questions cover all of the IRS reasonable cause criteria to one extent or another, so finding an answer to your personal or business situation that covers one or more of these questions is the key to a successful penalty abatement application.

Writing Your Penalty Abatement Request

You can use Form 843, *Claim for Refund and Request for Abatement* to apply for relief from penalties. However, as a tax practitioner, I never have, not even once. The reason is simply because the form only has room for about two sentences in order to explain WHY you are requesting the penalties to be removed. Therefore, you're going to end up writing a lengthy letter anyway that gets attached to the Form 843. Because of this, I simply write a letter for my clients that includes all the same information as the Form 843. My typical penalty abatement letter is 3 to 5 pages long, and some are even longer.

The format of a penalty abatement letter is fairly straightforward. When requesting a penalty abatement,

I suggest the following format:

1. Indicate the particular penalty types, tax periods, and penalty amounts that you are requesting to be reduced or removed.

2. Include a very brief introduction about who you are, where you live, your family size, and what you do. For a business, give a very brief description of your business, what it does, and how it does it.

3. Provide the background story to the event that caused the tax bills to go unpaid. Be sure to include very specific details, including names, dates, places, events, etc.

4. After explaining why the taxes weren't paid, explain what actions you took to correct the situation, including an explanation regarding the length of time it took to get the tax situation addressed.

5. For business taxes, explain why other business expenses were paid when the taxes were not.

6. Explain the current state of affairs, including the current status of your personal or business finances, and also the status of meeting your current tax obligations and how you've addressed the back tax liabilities

7. Sign your request under penalties of perjury.

Where To Send Penalty Abatement Requests

If you have or recently had a Revenue Officer assigned to you, send your penalty abatement request to that Revenue Officer.

If you do not have a Revenue Officer: Most of your IRS notices most likely come from one particular IRS service center. Make note of the address of that IRS center, and mail your request their to the attention of "Service Center Penalty Appeals Coordinator".

Penalty Abatement Review Process

Whether it is a Revenue Officer or the service center coordinator that reviews your request, they will make a determination regarding whether they believe your request meets reasonable cause criteria.

If it is determined that your application meets

reasonable cause criteria, the person reviewing your request will recommend removal of penalties for certain types and period, based on your circumstances. This recommendation will then be forwarded to a manager for final approval.

If your request is denied, you will be told so in writing. You are entitled to know the exact reason that your request was denied. If you are not supplied with this reason in the initial rejection letter, then you should call or write to that person to request it.

All penalty abatement denials have appeals rights. If your penalty abatement is denied for any reason, be sure that you exercise this right. Call our office if you need assistance with this appeal process, we'd be more than happy to help you with it.

This Book Is Just The Beginning

This book is intended to be just the beginning of a long and healthy relationship between the two of us. I'd like to invite you to visit my website at

www.CPAofThousandOaks.com

and receive my free report, *The Top Five Personal Tax-Saving IRS 'Secrets' For Surviving Tough Economic Times.* We'll also keep in touch with you on a regular basis-offering **Real World Personal Strategies** (*not just pie-in-the-sky theory*) and guidance for growing wealth, keeping sane in this world, and all-around personal development.

These will NOT be just ***tax tips*** (it's our job to take care of all that for you, after all). Sure, there will be tax items you'll need to know about that we'll send you info on, but I believe you'll find these notes to be interesting and useful on a variety of levels. Oh, and it's free.

Acknowledgements

Crystal Coleman, my girlfriend & office manager, you give me so much in so many ways. You have kept our team organized and orderly. You have helped us become so much more efficient and effective and I couldn't be happier to work with you everyday. This truly is a wonderful life.

My dog Roman for his unconditional love. I hope I can do as much for him as he does for me.

Paul Dubrow, my father, for so many of the obvious reasons, but mainly just for always being a really cool dad.

Dolby Dubrow, my mother, who has enlightened me in so many ways and has always been my #1 fan. Namaste.

Dakota Dubrow, my brother, for all those late night, wacky conversations, and teaching me to think "outside-the-box".

Jassen Bowman, my mentor, my friend, my coach. Thank you for showing me the light. I have learned so much from you.

Michel Manning: You are my all-star accountant. I am so grateful for you.

About The Author

Skylar Dubrow, CPA is totally a bro's bro. Besides being a CPA and an awesome guy, Skylar is the man when it comes to helping his clients pay the absolute least amount of tax and make sure their accounting is on the up and up.

In his spare time, you can usually find Skylar biking through the mountains of the Conejo Valley, getting inverted on his wakeboard at the local lake, or more often than not, power walking his neighborhood with Crystal and Roman listening to a good audio book.

When his name is mentioned anywhere, you'll always instantly hear 30 people scream in unison, "*That guy ROCKS!*"

Team up with Skylar today. You'll wish you had done so sooner. Visit CPAofThousandOaks.com or call (818) 889-7285 to connect with Skylar today.

www.ingramcontent.com/pod-product-compliance
Lightning Source LLC
Chambersburg PA
CBHW070820180526
45168CB00002B/688

* 9 7 8 1 5 0 7 8 0 6 8 9 0 *